George Brandon Saul.
Shoemakersville,
Pa.

July 21, 1917.

B. Brigid Brandon Saul
November 12, 1963

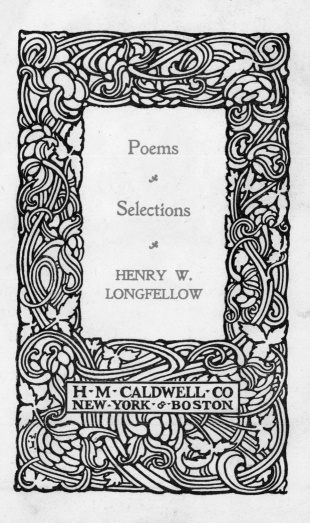

Poems

*

Selections

*

HENRY W.
LONGFELLOW

H·M·CALDWELL·CO
NEW·YORK·&·BOSTON

THE BELFRY OF BRUGES,
AND OTHER POEMS.

CARILLON.

In the ancient town of Bruges,
In the quaint old Flemish city,
As the evening shades descended,
Low and loud and sweetly blended,
Low at times and loud at times,
And changing like a poet's rhymes,
Rang the beautiful wild chimes
From the Belfry in the market
Of the ancient town of Bruges.

Then, with deep sonorous clangor
Calmly answering their sweet anger,
When the wrangling bells had ended,
Slowly struck the clock eleven,
And, from out the silent heaven,
Silence on the town descended.
Silence, silence everywhere,
On the earth and in the air,
Save that footsteps here and there

Of some burgher home returning,
By the street lamps faintly burning,
For a moment woke the echoes
Of the ancient town of Bruges.

But amid my broken slumbers
Still I heard those magic numbers,
As they loud proclaimed the flight
And stolen marches of the night;
Till their chimes in sweet collision
Mingled with each wandering vision,
Mingled with the fortune-telling
Gypsy-bands of dreams and fancies,
Which amid the waste expanses
Of the silent land of trances
Have their solitary dwelling;
All else seemed asleep in Bruges,
In the quaint old Flemish city.

And I thought how like these chimes
Are the poet's airy rhymes,
All his rhymes and roundelays,
His conceits, and songs, and ditties,
From the belfry of his brain,
Scattered downward, though in vain,
On the roofs and stones of cities!
For by night the drowsy ear
Under its curtains cannot hear,

And by day men go their ways,
Hearing the music as they pass,
But deeming it no more, alas !
Than the hollow sound of brass.

Yet perchance a sleepless wight,
Lodging at some humble inn
In the narrow lanes of life,
When the dusk and hush of night
Shut out the incessant din
Of daylight and its toil and strife,
May listen with a calm delight
To the poet's melodies,
Till he hears, or dreams he hears,
Intermingled with the song,
Thoughts that he has cherished long ;
Hears amid the chime and singing
The bells of his own village ringing,
And wakes, and finds his slumberous **eyes**
Wet with most delicious tears.

Thus dreamed I, as by night I lay
In Bruges, at the Fleur-de-Blé,
Listening with a wild delight
To the chimes that, through the night,
Rang their changes from the Belfry
Of that quaint old Flemish city.

THE BELFRY OF BRUGES.

In the market-place of Bruges stands the belfry
    old and brown;
Thrice consumed and thrice rebuilded, still it
    watches o'er the town.

As the summer morn was breaking, on that lofty
    tower I stood,
And the world threw off the darkness, like the
    weeds of widowhood.

Thick with towns and hamlets studded, and with
    streams and vapors gray,
Like a shield embossed with silver, round and
    vast the landscape lay.

At my feet the city slumbered. From its chim-
    neys, here and there,
Wreaths of snow-white smoke ascending, van-
    ished, ghost-like, into air.

Not a sound rose from the city at that early
    morning hour,
But I heard a heart of iron beating in the ancient
    tower.

From their nests beneath the rafters sang the
    swallows wild and high ;
And the world, beneath me sleeping, seemed
    more distant than the sky.

Then most musical and solemn, bringing back
    the olden times,
With their strange, unearthly changes rang the
    melancholy chimes,

Like the psalms from some old cloister, when
    the nuns sing in their choir ;
And the great bell tolled among them, like the
    chanting of a friar.

Visions of the days departed, shadowy phantoms
    filled my brain ;
They who live in history only seemed to walk
    the earth again ;

All the Foresters of Flanders, — mighty Baldwin
    Bras de Fer,
Lyderick du Bucq and Cressy Philip, Guy de
    Dampierre.

I beheld the pageants splendid that adorned
    those days of old ;
Stately dames, like queens attended, knights who
    bore the Fleece of Gold.

Lombard and Venetian merchants with deep-
    laden argosies;
Ministers from twenty nations: more than royal
    pomp and ease.

I beheld proud Maximilian, kneeling humbly on
    the ground;
I beheld the gentle Mary, hunting with her hawk
    and hound;

And her lighted bridal-chamber, where a duke
    slept with the queen,
And the armèd guard around them, and the
    sword unsheathed between.

I beheld the Flemish weavers, with Namur and
    Juliers bold,
Marching homeward from the bloody battle of
    the Spurs of Gold;

Saw the fight at Minnewater, saw the White
    Hoods moving west,
Saw great Artevelde victorious scale the Golden
    Dragon's nest.

And again the whiskered Spaniard all the land
    with terror smote;
And again the wild alarum sounded from the toc-
    sin's throat;

Till the bell of Ghent responded o'er lagoon and
     dike of sand,
" I am Roland!   I am Roland! there is victory
     in the land!"

Then the sound of drums aroused me.   The
     awakened city's roar
Chased the phantoms I had summoned back into
     their graves once more.

Hours had passed away like minutes; and, before
     I was aware,
Lo! the shadow of the belfry crossed the sun-
     illumined square.

" In the market-place of Bruges stands the
belfry old and brown."

MISCELLANEOUS.

MISCELLANEOUS.

A GLEAM OF SUNSHINE.

THIS is the place. Stand still, my steed,
   Let me review the scene,
And summon from the shadowy Past
   The forms that once have been.

The Past and Present here unite
   Beneath Time's flowing tide,
Like footprints hidden by a brook,
   But seen on either side.

Here runs the highway to the town;
   There the green lane descends,
Through which I walked to church with thee,
   O gentlest of my friends!

The shadow of the linden-trees
   Lay moving on the grass;
Between them and the moving boughs,
   A shadow, thou didst pass.

Thy dress was like the lilies,
  And thy heart as pure as they:
One of God's holy messengers
  Did walk with me that day.

I saw the branches of the trees
  Bend down thy touch to meet,
The clover-blossoms in the grass
  Rise up to kiss thy feet.

" Sleep, sleep to-day, tormenting cares,
  Of earth and folly born!"
Solemnly sang the village choir
  On that sweet Sabbath morn.

Through the closed blinds the golden sun
  Poured in a dusty beam,
Like the celestial ladder seen
  By Jacob in his dream.

And ever and anon, the wind,
  Sweet-scented with the hay,
Turned o'er the hymn-book's fluttering leaves
  That on the window lay.

Long was the good man's sermon,
  Yet it seemed not so to me;
For he spake of Ruth the beautiful,
  And still I thought of thee.

Long was the prayer he uttered,
  Yet it seemed not so to me;
For in my heart I prayed with him,
  And still I thought of thee.

But now, alas! the place seems changed;
  Thou art no longer here:
Part of the sunshine of the scene
  With thee did disappear.

Though thoughts, deep-rooted in my heart,
  Like pine-trees dark and high,
Subdue the light of noon, and breathe
  A low and ceaseless sigh;

This memory brightens o'er the past,
  As when the sun, concealed
Behind some cloud that near us hangs,
  Shines on a distant field.

————

THE ARSENAL AT SPRINGFIELD.

THIS is the Arsenal. From floor to ceiling,
  Like a huge organ, rise the burnished arms;
But from their silent pipes no anthem pealing
  Startles the villages with strange alarms.

Ah! what a sound will rise, how wild and dreary,
 When the death-angel touches those swift
   keys!
What loud lament and dismal Miserere
 Will mingle with their awful symphonies!

I hear even now the infinite fierce chorus,
 The cries of agony, the endless groan,
Which, through the ages that have gone before
   us,
 In long reverberations reach our own.

On helm and harness rings the Saxon hammer,
 Through Cimbric forest roars the Norseman's
   song,
And loud, amid the universal clamor,
 O'er distant deserts sounds the Tartar gong.

I hear the Florentine, who from his palace
 Wheels out his battle-bell with dreadful din,
And Aztec priests upon their teocallis
 Beat the wild war-drums made of serpent's
   skin;

The tumult of each sacked and burning village;
 The shout that every prayer for mercy drowns;
The soldiers' revels in the midst of pillage;
 The wail of famine in beleaguered towns;

The bursting shell, the gateway wrenched
    asunder,
  The rattling musketry, the clashing blade ;
And ever and anon, in tones of thunder,
  The diapason of the cannonade.

Is it, O man, with such discordant noises,
  With such accursed instruments as these,
Thou drownest Nature's sweet and kindly voices,
  And jarrest the celestial harmonies?

Were half the power, that fills the world with
    terror,
  Were half the wealth, bestowed on camps and
    courts,
Given to redeem the human mind from error,
  There were no need of arsenals or forts :

The warrior's name would be a name abhorred !
  And every nation, that should lift again
Its hand against a brother, on its forehead
  Would wear forevermore the curse of Cain !

Down the dark future, through long generations,
  The echoing sounds grow fainter and then
    cease ;
And like a bell, with solemn, sweet vibrations,
  I hear once more the voice of Christ say,
    " Peace ! "

Peace ! and no longer from its brazen portals
 The blast of War's great organ shakes the
  skies !
But beautiful as songs of the immortals,
 The holy melodies of love arise.

———

NUREMBERG.

In the valley of the Pegnitz, where across broad
  meadow-lands
Rise the blue Franconian mountains, Nuremberg,
  the ancient, stands.

Quaint old town of toil and traffic, quaint old
  town of art and song,
Memories haunt thy pointed gables like the rooks
  that round them throng :

Memories of the Middle Ages, when the empe-
  rors, rough and bold,
Had their dwelling in thy castle, time-defying,
  centuries old ;

And thy brave and thrifty burghers boasted, in
  their uncouth rhyme,
That their great imperial city stretched its hand
  through every clime.

NUREMBERG.

In the court-yard of the castle, bound with many
    an iron band,
Stands the mighty linden planted by Queen
    Cunigunde's hand;

On the square the oriel window, where in old
    heroic days
Sat the poet Melchior singing Kaiser Maximil-
    ian's praise.

Everywhere I see around me rise the wondrous
    world of Art:
Fountains wrought with richest sculpture stand-
    ing in the common mart;

And above cathedral doorways saints and bishops
    carved in stone,
By a former age commissioned as apostles to our
    own.

In the church of sainted Sebald sleeps enshrined
    his holy dust,
And in bronze the Twelve Apostles guard from
    age to age their trust;

In the church of sainted Lawrence stands a pix
    of sculpture rare,
Like the foamy sheaf of fountains, rising through
    the painted air.

Here, when Art was still religion, with a simple,
    reverent heart,
Lived and labored Albrecht Dürer, the Evangel-
    ist of Art;

Hence in silence and in sorrow, toiling still with
    busy hand,
Like an emigrant he wandered, seeking for the
    Better Land.

Emigravit is the inscription on the tomb-stone
    where he lies;
Dead he is not, but departed, — for the artist
    never dies.

Fairer seems the ancient city, and the sunshine
    seems more fair,
That he once has trod its pavement, that he once
    has breathed its air!

Through these streets so broad and stately, these
    obscure and dismal lanes,
Walked of yore the Mastersingers, chanting rude
    poetic strains.

From remote and sunless suburbs came they to
    the friendly guild,
Building nests in Fame's great temple, as in
    spouts the swallows build.

As the weaver plied the shuttle, wove he too the
    mystic rhyme,
And the smith his iron measures hammered to
    the anvil's chime;

Thanking God, whose boundless wisdom makes
    the flowers of poesy bloom
In the forge's dust and cinders, in the tissues of
    the loom.

Here Hans Sachs, the cobbler-poet, laureate of
    the gentle craft,
Wisest of the Twelve Wise Masters, in huge
    folios sang and laughed.

But his house is now an ale-house, with a nicely
    sanded floor,
And a garland in the window, and his face above
    the door;

Painted by some humble artist, as in Adam
    Puschman's song,
As the old man gray and dove-like, with his
    great beard white and long.

And at night the swart mechanic comes to drown
    his cark and care,
Quaffing ale from pewter tankards, in the mas-
    ter's antique chair.

Vanished is the ancient splendor, and before my
    dreamy eye
Wave these mingled shapes and figures, like a
    faded tapestry.

Not thy Councils, not thy Kaisers, win for thee
    the world's regard ;
But thy painter, Albrecht Dürer, and Hans Sachs
    thy cobbler-bard.

Thus, O Nuremberg, a wanderer from a region
    far away,
As he paced thy streets and court-yards, sang in
    thought his careless lay :

Gathering from the pavement's crevice, as a
    floweret of the soil,
The nobility of labor, — the long pedigree of
    toil.

———

RAIN IN SUMMER.

How beautiful is the rain !
After the dust and heat,
In the broad and fiery street,
In the narrow lane,
How beautiful is the rain !

RAIN IN SUMMER.

How it clatters along the roofs,
Like the tramp of hoofs!
How it gushes and struggles out
From the throat of the overflowing spout!

Across the window-pane
It pours and pours;
And swift and wide,
With a muddy tide,
Like a river down the gutter roars
The rain, the welcome rain!

The sick man from his chamber looks
At the twisted brooks;
He can feel the cool
Breath of each little pool;
His fevered brain
Grows calm again,
And he breathes a blessing on the rain.

From the neighboring school
Come the boys,
With more than their wonted noise
And commotion;
And down the wet streets
Sail their mimic fleets,
Till the treacherous pool
Ingulfs them in its whirling
And turbulent ocean.

In the country, on every side,
Where far and wide,
Like a leopard's tawny and spotted **hide**,
Stretches the plain,
To the dry grass and the dryer **grain**
How welcome is the rain!

In the furrowed land
The toilsome and patient oxen **stand**;
Lifting the yoke-encumbered head,
With their dilated nostrils spread,
They silently inhale
The clover-scented gale,
And the vapors that arise
From the well-watered and smoking **soil**.
For this rest in the furrow after toil
Their large and lustrous eyes
Seem to thank the Lord,
More than man's spoken word.

Near at hand,
From under the sheltering **trees**,
The farmer sees
His pastures, and his fields of **grain**,
As they bend their tops
To the numberless beating **drops**
Of the incessant rain.

He counts it as no sin
That he sees therein
Only his own thrift and gain.

These, and far more than these,
The Poet sees!
He can behold
Aquarius old
Walking the fenceless fields of air;
And from each ample fold
Of the clouds about him rolled
Scattering everywhere
The showery rain,
As the farmer scatters his grain.

He can behold
Things manifold
That have not yet been wholly told,—
Have not been wholly sung nor said.
For his thought, that never stops,
Follows the water-drops
Down to the graves of the dead,
Down through chasms and gulfs profound,
To the dreary fountain-head
Of lakes and rivers underground;
And sees them, when the rain is done,
On the bridge of colors seven
Climbing up once more to heaven,
Opposite the setting sun.

Thus the Seer,
With vision clear,
Sees forms appear and disappear,
In the perpetual round of strange,
Mysterious change
From birth to death, from death to birth,
From earth to heaven, from heaven to earth;
Till glimpses more sublime
Of things, unseen before,
Unto his wondering eyes reveal
The Universe, as an immeasurable wheel
Turning forevermore
In the rapid and rushing river of Time.

THE NORMAN BARON.

Dans les moments de la vie où la réflexion devient plus calme
et plus profonde, où l'intérêt et l'avarice parlent moins haut que
la raison, dans les instants de chagrin domestique, de maladie,
et de péril de mort, les nobles se repentirent de posséder des
serfs, comme d'une chose peu agréable à Dieu, qui avait créé
tous les hommes à son image.

THIERRY, *Conquête de l'Angleterre.*

In his chamber, weak and dying,
Was the Norman baron lying;
Loud, without, the tempest thundered,
And the castle-turret shook.

In this fight was Death the gainer,
Spite of vassal and retainer,
And the lands his sires had plundered,
    Written in the Doomsday Book.

By his bed a monk was seated,
Who in humble voice repeated
Many a prayer and pater-noster,
    From the missal on his knee;

And, amid the tempest pealing,
Sounds of bells came faintly stealing,
Bells, that from the neighboring kloster
    Rang for the Nativity.

In the hall, the serf and vassal
Held, that night, their Christmas wassail;
Many a carol, old and saintly,
    Sang the minstrels and the waits;

And so loud these Saxon gleemen
Sang to slaves the songs of freemen,
That the storm was heard but faintly,
    Knocking at the castle-gates.

Till at length the lays they chanted
Reached the chamber terror-haunted,
Where the monk, with accents holy,
    Whispered at the baron's ear.

Tears upon his eyelids glistened,
As he paused awhile and listened,
And the dying baron slowly
    Turned his weary head to hear.

" Wassail for the kingly stranger
Born and cradled in a manger !
King, like David, priest, like Aaron,
    Christ is born to set us free !"

And the lightning showed the sainted
Figures on the casement painted,
And exclaimed the shuddering baron,
    " Miserere, Domine !"

In that hour of deep contrition
He beheld, with clearer vision,
Through all outward show and fashion,
    Justice, the Avenger, rise.

All the pomp of earth had vanished,
Falsehood and deceit were banished,
Reason spake more loud than passion,
    And the truth wore no disguise.

Every vassal of his banner,
Every serf born to his manor,
All those wronged and wretched creatures,
    By his hand were freed again.

And, as on the sacred missal
He recorded their dismissal,
Death relaxed his iron features,
    And the monk replied, " Amen ! "

Many centuries have been numbered
Since in death the baron slumbered
By the convent's sculptured portal,
    Mingling with the common dust :

But the good deed, through the ages
Living in historic pages,
Brighter grows and gleams immortal,
    Unconsumed by moth or rust.

TO A CHILD.

DEAR child ! how radiant on thy mother's knee,
With merry-making eyes and jocund smiles,
Thou gazest at the painted tiles,
Whose figures grace,
With many a grotesque form and face,
The ancient chimney of thy nursery !
The lady with the gay macaw,
The dancing girl, the grave bashaw
With bearded lip and chin ;
And, leaning idly o'er his gate,
Beneath the imperial fan of state,
The Chinese mandarin.

With what a look of proud command
Thou shakest in thy little hand
The coral rattle with its silver bells,
Making a merry tune!
Thousands of years in Indian seas
That coral grew, by slow degrees,
Until some deadly and wild monsoon
Dashed it on Coromandel's sand!
Those silver bells
Reposed of yore,
As shapeless ore,
Far down in the deep-sunken wells
Of darksome mines,
In some obscure and sunless place,
Beneath huge Chimborazo's base,
Or Potosí's o'erhanging pines!
And thus for thee, O little child,
Through many a danger and escape,
The tall ships passed the stormy cape;
For thee in foreign lands remote,
Beneath a burning, tropic clime,
The Indian peasant, chasing the wild goat,
Himself as swift and wild,
In falling, clutched the frail arbute,
The fibres of whose shallow root,
Uplifted from the soil, betrayed
The silver veins beneath it laid,
The buried treasure of the miser, Time.

TO A CHILD.

But, lo! thy door is left ajar!
Thou hearest footsteps from afar!
And, at the sound,
Thou turnest round
With quick and questioning eyes,
Like one, who, in a foreign land,
Beholds on every hand
Some source of wonder and surprise!
And, restlessly, impatiently,
Thou strivest, strugglest, to be free.
The four walls of thy nursery
Are now like prison walls to thee.
No more thy mother's smiles,
No more the painted tiles,
Delight thee, nor the playthings on the floor,
That won thy little, beating heart before;
Thou strugglest for the open door.

Through these once solitary halls
Thy pattering footstep falls.
The sound of thy merry voice,
Makes the old walls
Jubilant, and they rejoice
With the joy of thy young heart,
O'er the light of whose gladness
No shadows of sadness
From the sombre background of memory start.
Once, ah, once, within these walls,

One whom memory oft recalls,
The Father of his Country, dwelt.
And yonder meadows broad and damp
The fires of the besieging camp
Encircled with a burning belt.
Up and down these echoing stairs,
Heavy with the weight of cares,
Sounded his majestic tread;
Yes, within this very room
Sat he in those hours of gloom,
Weary both in heart and head.

But what are these grave thoughts to thee?
Out, out! into the open air!
Thy only dream is liberty,
Thou carest little how or where.
I see thee eager at thy play,
Now shouting to the apples on the tree,
With cheeks as round and red as they;
And now among the yellow stalks,
Among the flowering shrubs and plants,
As restless as the bee.
Along the garden walks,
The tracks of thy small carriage-wheels I trace;
And see at every turn how they efface
Whole villages of sand-roofed tents,
That rise like golden domes
Above the cavernous and secret homes

Of wandering and nomadic tribes of ants.
Ah, cruel little Tamerlane,
Who, with thy dreadful reign,
Dost persecute and overwhelm
These hapless Troglodytes of thy realm!
What! tired already! with those suppliant looks,
And voice more beautiful than a poet's books,
Or murmuring sound of water as it flows,
Thou comest back to parley with repose!
This rustic seat in the old apple-tree,
With its o'erhanging golden canopy
Of leaves illuminate with autumnal hues,
And shining with the argent light of dews,
Shall for a season be our place of rest.
Beneath us, like an oriole's pendent nest,
From which the laughing birds have taken wing,
By thee abandoned, hangs thy vacant swing.
Dream-like the waters of the river gleam;
A sailless vessel drops adown the stream,
And like it, to a sea as wide and deep,
Thou driftest gently down the tides of sleep.

O child! O new-born denizen
Of life's great city! on thy head
The glory of the morn is shed,
Like a celestial benison!
Here at the portal thou dost stand,
And with thy little hand

Thou openest the mysterious gate
Into the future's undiscovered land.
I see its valves expand,
As at the touch of Fate!
Into those realms of love and hate,
Into that darkness blank and drear,
By some prophetic feeling taught,
I launch the bold, adventurous thought,
Freighted with hope and fear;
As upon subterranean streams,
In caverns unexplored and dark,
Men sometimes launch a fragile bark,
Laden with flickering fire,
And watch its swift-receding beams,
Until at length they disappear,
And in the distant dark expire.

By what astrology of fear or hope
Dare I to cast thy horoscope!
Like the new moon thy life appears;
A little strip of silver light,
And widening outward into night
The shadowy disk of future years;
And yet upon its outer rim,
A luminous circle, faint and dim,
And scarcely visible to us here,
Rounds and completes the perfect sphere;
A prophecy and intimation,

TO A CHILD.

A pale and feeble adumbration,
Of the great world of light, that lies
Behind all human destinies.

Ah! if thy fate, with anguish fraught,
Should be to wet the dusty soil
With the hot tears and sweat of toil, —
To struggle with imperious thought,
Until the overburdened brain,
Weary with labor, faint with pain,
Like a jarred pendulum, retain
Only its motion, not its power, —
Remember, in that perilous hour,
When most afflicted and oppressed,
From labor there shall come forth rest.

And if a more auspicious fate
On thy advancing steps await,
Still let it ever be thy pride
To linger by the laborer's side;
With words of sympathy or song
To cheer the dreary march along
Of the great army of the poor,
O'er desert sand, o'er dangerous moor.
Nor to thyself the task shall be
Without reward; for thou shalt learn
The wisdom early to discern
True beauty in utility;
As great Pythagoras of yore,

Standing beside the blacksmith's door,
And hearing the hammers, as they smote
The anvils with a different note,
Stole from the varying tones, that hung
Vibrant on every iron tongue,
The secret of the sounding wire,
And formed the seven-chorded lyre.

Enough! I will not play the Seer;
I will no longer strive to ope
The mystic volume, where appear
The herald Hope, forerunning Fear,
And Fear, the pursuivant of Hope.
Thy destiny remains untold;
For, like Acestes' shaft of old,
The swift thought kindles as it flies,
And burns to ashes in the skies.

THE OCCULTATION OF ORION.

I SAW, as in a dream sublime,
The balance in the hand of Time.
O'er East and West its beam impended;
And day, with all its hours of light,
Was slowly sinking out of sight,
While, opposite, the scale of night
Silently with the stars ascended.

Like the astrologers of eld,
In that bright vision I beheld
Greater and deeper mysteries.
I saw, with its celestial keys,
Its chords of air, its frets of fire,
The Samian's great Æolian lyre,
Rising through all its sevenfold bars,
From earth unto the fixed stars.
And through the dewy atmosphere,
Not only could I see, but hear,
Its wondrous and harmonious strings,
In sweet vibration, sphere by sphere,
From Dian's circle light and near,
Onward to vaster and wider rings,
Where, chanting through his beard of snows,
Majestic, mournful, Saturn goes,
And down the sunless realms of space
Reverberates the thunder of his bass.

Beneath the sky's triumphal arch
This music sounded like a march,
And with its chorus seemed to be
Preluding some great tragedy.
Sirius was rising in the east;
And, slow ascending one by one,
The kindling constellations shone.
Begirt with many a blazing star,
Stood the great giant Algebar,

Orion, hunter of the beast!
His sword hung gleaming by his side,
And, on his arm, the lion's hide
Scattered across the midnight air
The golden radiance of its hair.

The moon was pallid, but not faint;
And beautiful as some fair saint,
Serenely moving on her way
In hours of trial and dismay.
As if she heard the voice of God,
Unharmed with naked feet she trod
Upon the hot and burning stars,
As on the glowing coals and bars,
That were to prove her strength, and try
Her holiness and her purity.

Thus moving on, with silent pace,
And triumph in her sweet, pale face,
She reached the station of Orion.
Aghast he stood in strange alarm!
And suddenly from his outstretched arm
Down fell the red skin of the lion
Into the river at his feet.
His mighty club no longer beat
The forehead of the bull; but he
Reeled as of yore beside the sea,
When, blinded by Œnopion,

He sought the blacksmith at his forge,
And, climbing up the mountain gorge,
Fixed his blank eyes upon the sun.

Then, through the silence overhead,
An angel with a trumpet said,
" Forevermore, forevermore,
The reign of violence is o'er!"
And, like an instrument that flings
Its music on another's strings,
The trumpet of the angel cast
Upon the heavenly lyre its blast,
And on from sphere to sphere the words
Re-echoed down the burning chords, —
" Forevermore, forevermore,
The reign of violence is o'er!"

THE BRIDGE.

I STOOD on the bridge at midnight,
    As the clocks were striking the hour,
And the moon rose o'er the city,
    Behind the dark church-tower.

I saw her bright reflection
    In the waters under me,
Like a golden goblet falling
    And sinking into the sea.

And far in the hazy distance
  Of that lovely night in June,
The blaze of the flaming furnace
  Gleamed redder than the moon.

Among the long, black rafters,
  The wavering shadows lay,
And the current that came from the ocean
  Seemed to lift and bear them away;

As, sweeping and eddying through them,
  Rose the belated tide,
And, streaming into the moonlight,
  The seaweed floated wide.

And like those waters rushing
  Among the wooden piers,
A flood of thoughts came o'er me
  That filled my eyes with tears.

How often, O how often,
  In the days that had gone by,
I had stood on that bridge at midnight
  And gazed on that wave and sky!

How often, O how often,
  I had wished that the ebbing tide
Would bear me away on its bosom
  O'er the ocean wild and wide!

For my heart was hot and restless,
  And my life was full of care,
And the burden laid upon me
  Seemed greater than I could bear.

But now it has fallen from me,
  It is buried in the sea;
And only the sorrow of others
  Throws its shadow over me.

Yet whenever I cross the river
  On its bridge with wooden piers,
Like the odor of brine from the ocean
  Comes the thought of other years.

And I think how many thousands
  Of care-encumbered men,
Each bearing his burden of sorrow,
  Have crossed the bridge since then.

I see the long procession
  Still passing to and fro,
The young heart hot and restless,
  And the old subdued and slow!

And forever and forever,
  As long as the river flows,
As long as the heart has passions,
  As long as life has woes;

The moon and its broken reflection
And its shadows shall appear,
As the symbol of love in heaven,
And its wavering image here.

TO THE DRIVING CLOUD.

GLOOMY and dark art thou, O chief of the
mighty Omahas;
Gloomy and dark as the driving cloud, whose
name thou hast taken!
Wrapt in thy scarlet blanket, I see thee stalk
through the city's
Narrow and populous streets, as once by the
margin of rivers
Stalked those birds unknown, that have left us
only their footprints.
What, in a few short years, will remain of thy
race but the footprints?
How canst thou walk these streets, who hast
trod the green turf of the prairies?
How canst thou breathe this air, who hast
breathed the sweet air of the mountains?
Ah! 'tis in vain that with lordly looks of disdain
thou dost challenge
Looks of disdain in return, and question these
walls and these pavements,

268

Claiming the soil for thy hunting-grounds, while
    down-trodden millions
Starve in the garrets of Europe, and cry from its
    caverns that they, too,
Have been created heirs of the earth, and claim
    its division!

Back, then, back to thy woods in the regions
    west of the Wabash!
There as a monarch thou reignest. In autumn
    the leaves of the maple
Pave the floors of thy palace-halls with gold, and
    in summer
Pine-trees waft through its chambers the odorous
    breath of their branches.
There thou art strong and great, a hero, a tamer
    of horses!
There thou chasest the stately stag on the banks
    of the Elkhorn,
Or by the roar of the Running-Water, or where
    the Omaha
Calls thee, and leaps through the wild ravine
    like a brave of the Blackfeet!

Hark! what murmurs arise from the heart of
    those mountainous deserts?
Is it the cry of the Foxes and Crows, or the
    mighty Behemoth,

Who, unharmed, on his tusks once caught the
    bolts of the thunder,
And now lurks in his lair to destroy the race of
    the red man?
Far more fatal to thee and thy race than the
    Crows and the Foxes,
Far more fatal to thee and thy race than the
    tread of Behemoth,
Lo! the big thunder-canoe, that steadily breasts
    the Missouri's
Merciless current! and yonder, afar on the
    prairies, the camp-fires
Gleam through the night; and the cloud of dust
    in the gray of the daybreak
Marks not the buffalo's track, nor the Mandan's
    dexterous horse-race;
It is a caravan, whitening the desert where dwell
    the Camanches!
Ha! how the breath of these Saxons and Celts,
    like the blast of the east-wind,
Drifts evermore to the west the scanty smokes
    of thy wigwams!

SONGS.

SONGS.

SEAWEED.

WHEN descends on the Atlantic
    The gigantic
Storm-wind of the equinox,
Landward in his wrath he scourges
    The toiling surges,
Laden with seaweed from the rocks:

From Bermuda's reefs; from edges
    Of sunken ledges,
In some far-off, bright Azore;
From Bahama, and the dashing,
    Silver-flashing
Surges of San Salvador;

From the tumbling surf, that buries
    The Orkneyan skerries,
Answering the hoarse Hebrides;
And from wrecks of ships, and drifting
    Spars, uplifting
On the desolate, rainy seas; —

Ever drifting, drifting, drifting
    On the shifting

SEAWEED.

Currents of the restless main;
Till in sheltered coves, and reaches
    Of sandy beaches,
All have found repose again.

So when storms of wild emotion
    Strike the ocean
Of the poet's soul, erelong
From each cave and rocky fastness,
    In its vastness,
Floats some fragment of a song:

From the far-off isles enchanted,
    Heaven has planted
With the golden fruit of Truth;
From the flashing surf, whose vision
    Gleams Elysian
In the tropic clime of Youth;

From the strong Will, and the Endeavor
    That forever
Wrestles with the tides of Fate;
From the wreck of Hopes far-scattered,
    Tempest-shattered,
Floating waste and desolate; —

Ever drifting, drifting, drifting
    On the shifting
Currents of the restless heart;

Till at length in books recorded,
    They, like hoarded
Household words, no more depart.

THE DAY IS DONE.

THE day is done, and the darkness
    Falls from the wings of Night,
As a feather is wafted downward
    From an eagle in his flight.

I see the lights of the village
    Gleam through the rain and the mist,
And a feeling of sadness comes o'er me
    That my soul cannot resist :

A feeling of sadness and longing,
    That is not akin to pain,
And resembles sorrow only
    As the mist resembles the rain.

Come, read to me some poem,
    Some simple and heartfelt lay,
That shall soothe this restless feeling,
    And banish the thoughts of day.

Not from the grand old masters,
    Not from the bards sublime,

Whose distant footsteps echo
  Through the corridors of Time.

For, like strains of martial music,
  Their mighty thoughts suggest
Life's endless toil and endeavor;
  And to-night I long for rest.

Read from some humbler poet,
  Whose songs gushed from his heart,
As showers from the clouds of summer,
  Or tears from the eyelids start;

Who, through long days of labor,
  And nights devoid of ease,
Still heard in his soul the music
  Of wonderful melodies.

Such songs have power to quiet
  The restless pulse of care,
And come like the benediction
  That follows after prayer.

Then read from the treasured volume
  The poem of thy choice,
And lend to the rhyme of the poet
  The beauty of thy voice.

And the night shall be filled with music,
  And the cares, that infest the day,

Shall fold their tents, like the Arabs,
  And as silently steal away.

———

AFTERNOON IN FEBRUARY.

THE day is ending,
The night is descending;
The marsh is frozen,
  The river dead.

Through clouds like ashes
The red sun flashes
On village windows
  That glimmer red.

The snow recommences;
The buried fences
Mark no longer
  The road o'er the plain;

While through the meadows,
Like fearful shadows,
Slowly passes
  A funeral train.

The bell is pealing,
And every feeling
Within me responds
  To the dismal knell;

Shadows are trailing,
My heart is bewailing
And tolling within
  Like a funeral bell.

TO AN OLD DANISH SONG-BOOK.

WELCOME, my old friend,
Welcome to a foreign fireside,
While the sullen gales of autumn
Shake the windows.

The ungrateful world
Has, it seems, dealt harshly with thee,
Since, beneath the skies of Denmark,
First I met thee.

There are marks of age,
There are thumb-marks on thy margin,
Made by hands that clasped thee rudely,
At the ale-house.

Soiled and dull thou art;
Yellow are thy time-worn pages,
As the russet, rain-molested
Leaves of autumn.

278

TO AN OLD DANISH SONG-BOOK.

Thou art stained with wine
Scattered from hilarious goblets,
As the leaves with the libations
Of Olympus.

Yet dost thou recall
Days departed, half-forgotten,
When in dreamy youth I wandered
By the Baltic, —

When I paused to hear
The old ballad of King Christian
Shouted from suburban taverns
In the twilight.

Thou recallest bards,
Who, in solitary chambers,
And with hearts by passion wasted,
Wrote thy pages.

Thou recallest homes
Where thy songs of love and friendship
Made the gloomy Northern winter
Bright as summer.

Once some ancient Scald,
In his bleak, ancestral Iceland,
Chanted staves of these old ballads
To the Vikings.

Once in Elsinore,
At the court of old King Hamlet,
Yorick and his boon companions
Sang these ditties.

Once Prince Frederick's Guard
Sang them in their smoky barracks; —
Suddenly the English cannon
Joined the chorus!

Peasants in the field,
Sailors on the roaring ocean,
Students, tradesmen, pale mechanics,
All have sung them.

Thou hast been their friend;
They, alas! have left thee friendless!
Yet at least by one warm fireside
Art thou welcome.

And, as swallows build
In these wide, old-fashioned chimneys,
So thy twittering songs shall nestle
In my bosom, —

Quiet, close, and warm,
Sheltered from all molestation,
And recalling by their voices
Youth and travel.

WALTER VON DER VOGELWEID.

VOGELWEID the Minnesinger,
  When he left this world of ours,
Laid his body in the cloister,
  Under Würtzburg's minster towers.

And he gave the monks his treasures,
  Gave them all with this behest:
They should feed the birds at noontide
  Daily on his place of rest;

Saying, " From these wandering minstrels
  I have learned the art of song;
Let me now repay the lessons
  They have taught so well and long."

Thus the bard of love departed;
  And, fulfilling his desire,
On his tomb the birds were feasted
  By the children of the choir.

Day by day, o'er tower and turret,
  In foul weather and in fair,
Day by day, in vastly numbers,
  Flocked the poets of the air.

On the tree whose heavy branches
  Overshadowed all the place,

On the pavement, on the tombstone,
　On the poet's sculptured face,

On the cross-bars of each window,
　On the lintel of each door,
They renewed the War of Wartburg,
　Which the bard had fought before.

There they sang their merry carols,
　Sang their lauds on every side;
And the name their voices uttered
　Was the name of Vogelweid.

Till at length the portly abbot
　Murmured, "Why this waste of food?
Be it changed to loaves henceforward
　For our fasting brotherhood."

Then in vain o'er tower and turret,
　From the walls and woodland nests,
When the minster bells rang noontide,
　Gathered the unwelcomed guests.

Then in vain, with cries discordant,
　Clamorous round the Gothic spire,
Screamed the feathered Minnesingers
　For the children of the choir.

Time has long effaced the inscriptions
 On the cloister's funeral stones,
And tradition only tells us
 Where repose the poet's bones.

But around the vast cathedral,
 By sweet echoes multiplied,
Still the birds repeat the legend,
 And the name of Vogelweid.

———

DRINKING SONG.

INSCRIPTION FOR AN ANTIQUE PITCHER.

COME, old friend! sit down and listen!
 From the pitcher, placed between us,
How the waters laugh and glisten
 In the head of old Silenus!

Old Silenus, bloated, drunken,
 Led by his inebriate Satyrs;
On his breast his head is sunken,
 Vacantly he leers and chatters.

Fauns with youthful Bacchus follow;
 Ivy crowns that brow supernal
As the forehead of Apollo,
 And possessing youth eternal.

283

Round about him, fair Bacchantes,
  Bearing cymbals, flutes, and thyrses,
Wild from Naxian groves, or Zante's
  Vineyards, sing delirious verses.

Thus he won, through all the nations,
  Bloodless victories, and the farmer
Bore, as trophies and oblations,
  Vines for banners, ploughs for armor.

Judged by no o'erzealous rigor,
  Much this mystic throng expresses;
Bacchus was the type of vigor,
  And Silenus of excesses.

These are ancient ethnic revels,
  Of a faith long since forsaken;
Now the Satyrs, changed to devils,
  Frighten mortals wine-o'ertaken.

Now to rivulets from the mountains
  Point the rods of fortune-tellers;
Youth perpetual dwells in fountains, —
  Not in flasks, and casks, and cellars.

Claudius, though he sang of flagons
  And huge tankards filled with Rhenish,
From that fiery blood of dragons
  Never would his own replenish.

Even Redi, though he chaunted
    Bacchus in the Tuscan valleys,
Never drank the wine he vaunted
    In his dithyrambic sallies.

Then with water fill the pitcher
    Wreathed about with classic fables;
Ne'er Falernian threw a richer
    Light upon Lucullus' tables.

Come, old friend, sit down and listen!
    As it passes thus between us,
How its wavelets laugh and glisten
    In the head of old Silenus!

THE OLD CLOCK ON THE STAIRS.

L'éternité est une pendule, dont le balancier dit et redit sans cesse ces deux mots seulement, dans le silence des tombeaux: "Toujours! jamais! Jamais! toujours!"

                         JACQUES BRIDAINE.

SOMEWHAT back from the village street
Stands the old-fashioned country-seat.
Across its antique portico
Tall poplar trees their shadows throw;
And from its station in the hall
An ancient timepiece says to all, —
        "Forever — never!
        Never — forever!"

Half-way up the stairs it stands,
And points and beckons with its hands
From its case of massive oak,
Like a monk, who, under his cloak,
Crosses himself, and sighs, alas!
With sorrowful voice to all who pass, —
        " Forever — never!
        Never — forever!"

By day its voice is low and light;
But in the silent dead of night,
Distinct as a passing footstep's fall,
It echoes along the vacant hall,
Along the ceiling, along the floor,
And seems to say, at each chamber-door,
        " Forever — never!
        Never — forever!"

Through days of sorrow and of mirth,
Through days of death and days of birth,
Through every swift vicissitude
Of changeful time, unchanged it has stood,
And as if, like God, it all things saw,
It calmly repeats those words of awe, —
        " Forever — never!
        Never — forever!"

In that mansion used to be
Free-hearted Hospitality;

His great fires up the chimney roared;
The stranger feasted at his board;
But, like the skeleton at the feast,
That warning timepiece never ceased, —
       " Forever — never!
       Never — forever!"

There groups of merry children played,
There youths and maidens dreaming strayed;
O precious hours! O golden prime,
And affluence of love and time!
Even as a miser counts his gold,
Those hours the ancient timepiece told, —
       " Forever — never!
       Never — forever!"

From that chamber, clothed in white,
The bride came forth on her wedding night;
There, in that silent room below,
The dead lay in his shroud of snow;
And in the hush that followed the prayer,
Was heard the old clock on the stair, —
       " Forever — never!
       Never — forever!"

All are scattered now and fled,
Some are married, some are dead;
And when I ask, with throbs of pain,
" Ah! when shall they all meet again?"

As in the days long since gone by,
The ancient timepiece makes reply, —
      " Forever — never !
      Never — forever ! "

Never here, forever there,
Where all parting, pain, and care,
And death, and time shall disappear, —
Forever there, but never here !
The horologe of Eternity
Sayeth this incessantly, —
      " Forever — never !
      Never — forever ! "

THE ARROW AND THE SONG.

I SHOT an arrow into the air,
It fell to earth, I knew not where ;
For, so swiftly it flew, the sight
Could not follow it in its flight.

I breathed a song into the air,
It fell to earth, I knew not where ;
For who has sight so keen and strong,
That it can follow the flight of song ?

Long, long afterward, in an oak
I found the arrow, still unbroke ;
And the song, from beginning to end,
I found again in the heart of a friend.

SONNETS.

SONNETS.

THE EVENING STAR.

Lo! in the painted oriel of the West,
   Whose panes the sunken sun incarnadines,
   Like a fair lady at her casement, shines
   The evening star, the star of love and rest!
And then anon she doth herself divest
   Of all her radiant garments, and reclines
   Behind the sombre screen of yonder pines,
   With slumber and soft dreams of love op-
      pressed.
O my beloved, my sweet Hesperus!
   My morning and my evening star of love!
   My best and gentlest lady! even thus,
As that fair planet in the sky above,
   Dost thou retire unto thy rest at night,
   And from thy darkened window fades **the**
      light.

AUTUMN.

Thou comest, Autumn, heralded by the rain,
   With banners, by great gales incessant fanned,
   Brighter than brightest silks of Samarcand,
   And stately oxen harnessed to thy wain!
Thou standest, like imperial Charlemagne,
   Upon thy bridge of gold; thy royal hand
   Outstretched with benedictions o'er the land,
   Blessing the farms through all thy vast do-
      main!
Thy shield is the red harvest moon, suspended
   So long beneath the heaven's o'erhanging
      eaves;
   Thy steps are by the farmer's prayers at-
      tended;
Like flames upon an altar shine the sheaves;
   And, following thee, in thy ovation splendid,
   Thine almoner, the wind, scatters the golden
      leaves!

––––––

DANTE.

Tuscan, that wanderest through the realms of
      gloom,
   With thoughtful pace, and sad, majestic eyes,
   Stern thoughts and awful from thy soul arise,
   Like Farinata from his fiery tomb.
Thy sacred song is like the trump of doom;

Yet in thy heart what human sympathies,
With soft compassion glows, as in the skies
The tender stars their clouded lamps relume!
Methinks I see thee stand, with pallid cheeks,
By Fra Hilario in his diocese,
As up the convent-walls, in golden streaks,
The ascending sunbeams mark the day's de-
 crease;
And, as he asks what there the stranger seeks,
Thy voice along the cloister whispers,
 "Peace!"

———

CURFEW.

I.

SOLEMNLY, mournfully,
 Dealing its dole,
The Curfew Bell
 Is beginning to toll.

Cover the embers,
 And put out the light;
Toil comes with the morning,
 And rest with the night.

Dark grow the windows,
 And quenched is the fire;
Sound fades into silence, —
 All footsteps retire.

No voice in the chambers,
　No sound in the hall!
Sleep and oblivion
　Reign over all!

II.

THE book is completed,
　And closed, like the day;
And the hand that has written it
　Lays it away.

Dim grow its fancies;
　Forgotten they lie:
Like coals in the ashes,
　They darken and die.

Song sinks into silence,
　The story is told,
The windows are darkened,
　The hearth-stone is cold.

Darker and darker
　The black shadows fall;
Sleep and oblivion
　Reign over all.

THE SEASIDE AND THE FIRE-
SIDE.

THE SEASIDE AND THE FIRE-
SIDE.

DEDICATION.

As one who, walking in the twilight gloom,
  Hears round about him voices as it darkens,
And seeing not the forms from which they come,
  Pauses from time to time, and turns and
    hearkens;

So walking here in twilight, O my friends!
  I hear your voices, softened by the distance,
And pause, and turn to listen, as each sends
  His words of friendship, comfort, and assist-
    ance.

If any thought of mine, or sung or told,
  Has ever given delight or consolation,
Ye have repaid me back a thousand-fold,
  By every friendly sign and salutation.

297

Thanks for the sympathies that ye have shown!
　Thanks for each kindly word, each silent
　　token,
That teaches me, when seeming most alone,
　Friends are around us, though no word be
　　spoken.

Kind messages, that pass from land to land;
　Kind letters, that betray the heart's deep his-
　　tory,
In which we feel the pressure of a hand, —
　One touch of fire, — and all the rest is mystery!

The pleasant books, that silently among
　Our household treasures take familiar places,
And are to us as if a living tongue
　Spake from the printed leaves or pictured faces!

Perhaps on earth I never shall behold,
　With eye of sense, your outward form and
　　semblance;
Therefore to me ye never will grow old,
　But live forever young in my remembrance.

Never grow old, nor change, nor pass away!
　Your gentle voices will flow on forever,
When life grows bare and tarnished with decay,
　As through a leafless landscape flows a river.

DEDICATION.

Not chance of birth or place has made us friends,
  Being oftentimes of different tongues and na-
    tions,
But the endeavor for the selfsame ends,
  With the same hopes, and fears, and aspira-
    tions.

Therefore I hope to join your seaside walk,
  Saddened, and mostly silent, with emotion;
Not interrupting with intrusive talk
  The grand, majestic symphonies of ocean.

Therefore I hope, as no unwelcome guest,
  At your warm fireside, when the lamps are
    lighted,
To have my place reserved among the rest,
  Nor stand as one unsought and uninvited!

BY THE SEASIDE.

BY THE SEASIDE.

THE BUILDING OF THE SHIP.

"BUILD me straight, O worthy Master!
  Stanch and strong, a goodly vessel,
That shall laugh at all disaster,
  And with wave and whirlwind wrestle!"

The merchant's word
Delighted the Master heard;
For his heart was in his work, and the heart
Giveth grace unto every Art.

A quiet smile played round his lips,
As the eddies and dimples of the tide
Play round the bows of ships,
That steadily at anchor ride.
And with a voice that was full of glee,
He answered, "Ere long we will launch
A vessel as goodly, and strong, and stanch,
As ever weathered a wintry sea!"

And first with nicest skill and art,
Perfect and finished in every part,
A little model the Master wrought,
Which should be to the larger plan
What the child is to the man,
Its counterpart in miniature;
That with a hand more swift and sure
The greater labor might be brought
To answer to his inward thought.
And as he labored, his mind ran o'er
The various ships that were built of yore,
And above them all, and strangest of all
Towered the Great Harry, crank and tall,
Whose picture was hanging on the wall,
With bows and stern raised high in air,
And balconies hanging here and there,
And signal lanterns and flags afloat,
And eight round towers, like those that frown
From some old castle, looking down
Upon the drawbridge and the moat.
And he said with a smile, "Our ship, I wis,
Shall be of another form than this!"

It was of another form, indeed;
Built for freight, and yet for speed,
A beautiful and gallant craft;
Broad in the beam, that the stress of the b's
Pressing down upon sail and mast,

Might not the sharp bows overwhelm;
Broad in the beam, but sloping aft
With graceful curve and slow degrees,
That she might be docile to the helm,
And that the currents of parted seas,
Closing behind, with mighty force,
Might aid and not impede her course.

In the ship-yard stood the Master,
    With the model of the vessel,
That should laugh at all disaster,
    And with wave and whirlwind wrestle!

Covering many a rood of ground,
Lay the timber piled around;
Timber of chestnut, and elm, and oak,
And scattered here and there, with these,
The knarred and crooked cedar knees;
Brought from regions far away,
From Pascagoula's sunny bay,
And the banks of the roaring Roanoke!
Ah! what a wondrous thing it is
To note how many wheels of toil
One thought, one word, can set in motion!
There's not a ship that sails the ocean,
But every climate, every soil,
Must bring its tribute, great or small,
And help to build the wooden wall!

The sun was rising o'er the sea,
And long the level shadows lay,
As if they, too, the beams would be
Of some great, airy argosy,
Framed and launched in a single day.
That silent architect, the sun,
Had hewn and laid them every one,
Ere the work of man was yet begun.
Beside the Master, when he spoke,
A youth, against an anchor leaning,
Listened, to catch his slightest meaning.
Only the long waves, as they broke
In ripples on the pebbly beach,
Interrupted the old man's speech.

Beautiful they were, in sooth,
The old man and the fiery youth!
The old man, in whose busy brain
Many a ship that sailed the main
Was modelled o'er and o'er again; —
The fiery youth, who was to be
The heir of his dexterity,
The heir of his house, and his daughter's hand,
When he had built and launched from land
What the elder head had planned.

"Thus," said he, "will we build this ship!
Lay square the blocks upon the slip,
And follow well this plan of mine.

Choose the timbers with greatest care;
Of all that is unsound beware;
For only what is sound and strong
To this vessel shall belong.
Cedar of Maine and Georgia pine
Here together shall combine.
A goodly frame, and a goodly fame,
And the UNION be her name!
For the day that gives her to the sea
Shall give my daughter unto thee!"

The Master's word
Enraptured the young man heard;
And as he turned his face aside,
With a look of joy and a thrill of pride,
Standing before
Her father's door,
He saw the form of his promised bride.
The sun shone on her golden hair,
And her cheek was glowing fresh and fair,
With the breath of morn and the soft sea air.
Like a beauteous barge was she,
Still at rest on the sandy beach,
Just beyond the billow's reach;
But he
Was the restless, seething, stormy sea!

Ah, how skilful grows the hand
That obeyeth Love's command!

It is the heart, and not the brain,
That to the highest doth attain,
And he who followeth Love's behest
Far excelleth all the rest!
Thus with the rising of the sun
Was the noble task begun,
And soon throughout the ship-yard's **bounds**
Were heard the intermingled sounds
Of axes and of mallets, plied
With vigorous arms on every side;
Plied so deftly and so well,
That, ere the shadows of evening fell,
The keel of oak for a noble ship,
Scarfed and bolted, straight and strong,
Was lying ready, and stretched along
The blocks, well placed upon the slip.
Happy, thrice happy, every one
Who sees his labor well begun,
And not perplexed and multiplied,
By idly waiting for time and tide!

And when the hot, long day was o'er,
The young man at the Master's door
Sat with the maiden, calm and still.
And within the porch, a little more
Removed beyond the evening chill,
The father sat, and told them tales
Of wrecks in the great September gales,

Of pirates upon the Spanish Main,
And ships that never came back again,
The chance and change of a sailor's life,
Want and plenty, rest and strife,
His roving fancy, like the wind,
That nothing can stay and nothing can bind,
And the magic charm of foreign lands,
With shadows of palms, and shining sands,
Where the tumbling surf,
O'er the coral reefs of Madagascar,
Washes the feet of the swarthy Lascar,
As he lies alone and asleep on the turf.
And the trembling maiden held her breath
At the tales of that awful, pitiless sea,
With all its terror and mystery,
The dim, dark sea, so like unto death,
That divides and yet unites mankind!
And whenever the old man paused, a gleam
From the bowl of his pipe would awhile illume
The silent group in the twilight gloom,
And thoughtful faces, as in a dream;
And for a moment one might mark
What had been hidden by the dark,
That the head of the maiden lay at rest,
Tenderly, on the young man's breast!

Day by day the vessel grew,
With timbers fashioned strong and true,

Stemson and keelson and sternson-knee,
Till, framed with perfect symmetry,
A skeleton ship rose up to view!
And around the bows and along the side
The heavy hammers and mallets plied,
Till after many a week, at length,
Wonderful for form and strength,
Sublime in its enormous bulk,
Loomed aloft the shadowy hulk!
And around it columns of smoke, upwreathing,
Rose from the boiling, bubbling, seething
Caldron, that glowed,
And overflowed
With the black tar, heated for the sheathing.
And amid the clamors
Of clattering hammers,
He who listened heard now and then
The song of the master and his men:—
"Build me straight, O worthy Master,
    Stanch and strong, a goodly vessel,
That shall laugh at all disaster,
    And with wave and whirlwind wrestle!"

With oaken brace and copper band,
Lay the rudder on the sand,
That, like a thought, should have control
Over the movement of the whole;
And near it the anchor, whose giant hand

Would reach down and grapple with the land,
And immovable and fast
Hold the great ship against the bellowing blast!
And at the bows an image stood,
By a cunning artist carved in wood,
With robes of white, that far behind
Seemed to be fluttering in the wind.
It was not shaped in a classic mould,
Not like a Nymph or Goddess of old,
Or Naiad rising from the water,
But modelled from the Master's daughter!
On many a dreary and misty night,
'Twill be seen by the rays of the signal light,
Speeding along through the rain and the dark,
Like a ghost in its snow-white sark,
The pilot of some phantom bark,
Guiding the vessel, in its flight,
By a path none other knows aright!
Behold, at last,
Each tall and tapering mast
Is swung into its place;
Shrouds and stays
Holding it firm and fast!

Long ago,
In the deer-haunted forests of Maine,
When upon mountain and plain
Lay the snow,

They fell, — those lordly pines!
Those grand, majestic pines!
'Mid shouts and cheers
The jaded steers,
Panting beneath the goad,
Dragged down the weary, winding road
Those captive kings so straight and tall,
To be shorn of their streaming hair,
And, naked and bare,
To feel the stress and the strain
Of the wind and the reeling main,
Whose roar
Would remind them forevermore
Of their native forests they should not see again.

And everywhere
The slender, graceful spars
Poise aloft in the air,
And at the mast-head,
White, blue, and red,
A flag unrolls the stripes and stars.
Ah! when the wanderer, lonely, friendless,
In foreign harbors shall behold
That flag unrolled
'Twill be as a friendly hand
Stretched out from his native land,
Filling his heart with memories sweet and end-
    less!

"With fleecy clouds the sky is blanched."

All those secret currents, that flow
With such resistless undertow,
And lift and drift, with terrible force,
The will from its moorings and its course.
Therefore he spake, and thus said he : —
" Like unto ships far off at sea,
Outward or homeward bound, are we.
Before, behind, and all around,
Floats and swings the horizon's bound,
Seems at its outer rim to rise
And climb the crystal wall of the skies,
And then again to turn and sink,
As if we could slide from its outer brink.
Ah ! it is not the sea,
It is not the sea that sinks and shelves,
But ourselves
That rock and rise
With endless and uneasy motion,
Now touching the very skies,
Now sinking into the depths of ocean.
Ah ! if our souls but poise and swing
Like the compass in its brazen ring,
Ever level and ever true
To the toil and the task we have to do,
We shall sail securely, and safely reach
The Fortunate Isles, on whose shining beach
The sights we see, and the sounds we hear,
Will be those of joy and not of fear ! "

Then the Master,
With a gesture of command,
Waved his hand;
And at the word,
Loud and sudden there was heard,
All around them and below,
The sound of hammers, blow on blow,
Knocking away the shores and spurs.
And see! she stirs!
She starts, — she moves, — she seems to feel
The thrill of life along her keel,
And, spurning with her foot the ground,
With one exulting, joyous bound,
She leaps into the ocean's arms!

And lo! from the assembled crowd
There rose a shout, prolonged and loud,
That to the ocean seemed to say,
"Take her, O bridegroom, old and gray,
Take her to thy protecting arms,
With all her youth and all her charms!"

How beautiful she is! How fair
She lies within those arms, that press
Her form with many a soft caress
Of tenderness and watchful care!
Sail forth into the sea, O ship!
Through wind and wave, right onward steer!

" My soul is full of longing
For the secret of the sea."

The moistened eye, the trembling lip,
Are not the signs of doubt or fear.
Sail forth into the sea of life,
O gentle, loving, trusting wife,
And safe from all adversity
Upon the bosom of that sea
Thy comings and thy goings be!
For gentleness and love and trust
Prevail o'er angry wave and gust;
And in the wreck of noble lives
Something immortal still survives!

Thou, too, sail on, O Ship of State!
Sail on, O UNION, strong and great!
Humanity with all its fears,
With all the hopes of future years,
Is hanging breathless on thy fate!
We know what Master laid thy keel,
What Workmen wrought thy ribs of steel,
Who made each mast, and sail, and rope,
What anvils rang, what hammers beat,
In what a forge and what a heat
Were shaped the anchors of thy hope!
Fear not each sudden sound and shock,
'Tis of the wave and not the rock;
'Tis but the flapping of the sail,
And not a rent made by the gale!
In spite of rock and tempest's roar,

In spite of false lights on the shore,
Sail on, nor fear to breast the sea!
Our hearts, our hopes, are all with thee,
Our hearts, our hopes, our prayers, **our tears,**
Our faith triumphant o'er our fears,
Are all with thee, — are all with thee!

————

THE EVENING STAR.

JUST above yon sandy bar,
　As the day grows fainter and dimmer,
Lonely and lovely, a single star
　Lights the air with a dusky glimmer.

Into the ocean faint and far
　Falls the trail of its golden splendor,
And the gleam of that single star
　Is ever refulgent, soft, and tender.

Chrysaor, rising out of the sea,
　Showed thus glorious and thus emulous,
Leaving the arms of Callirrhoe,
　Forever tender, soft, and tremulous.

Thus o'er the ocean faint and far
　Trailed the gleam of his falchion brightly;
Is it a God, or is it a star
　That, entranced, I gaze on nightly!

THE SECRET OF THE SEA.

Ah! what pleasant visions haunt me
  As I gaze upon the sea!
All the old romantic legends,
  All my dreams, come back to me.

Sails of silk and ropes of sandal,
  Such as gleam in ancient lore;
And the singing of the sailors,
  And the answer from the shore!

Most of all, the Spanish ballad
  Haunts me oft, and tarries long,
Of the noble Count Arnaldos
  And the sailor's mystic song.

Like the long waves on a sea-beach,
  Where the sand as silver shines,
With a soft, monotonous cadence,
  Flows its unrhymed lyric lines; —

Telling how the Count Arnaldos,
  With his hawk upon his hand,
Saw a fair and stately galley,
  Onward steering to the land; —

How he heard the ancient helmsman
  Chant a song so wild and clear,
That the sailing sea-bird slowly
  Poised upon the mast to hear,

Till his soul was full of longing
    And he cried, with impulse strong, —
"Helmsman! for the love of heaven,
    Teach me, too, that wondrous song!"

"Wouldst thou," — so the helmsman **answered,**
    "Learn the secret of the sea?
Only those who brave its dangers
    Comprehend its mystery!"

In each sail that skims the horizon,
    In each landward-blowing breeze,
I behold that stately galley,
    Hear those mournful melodies;

Till my soul is full of longing
    For the secret of the sea,
And the heart of the great ocean
    Sends a thrilling pulse through me.

———

TWILIGHT.

THE twilight is sad and cloudy,
    The wind blows wild and free,
And like the wings of the sea-birds
    Flash the white caps of the sea.

But in the fisherman's cottage
   There shines a ruddier light,
And a little face at the window
   Peers out into the night.

Close, close it is pressed to the **window,**
   As if those childish eyes
Were looking into the darkness,
   To see some form arise.

And a woman's waving shadow
   Is passing to and fro,
Now rising to the ceiling,
   Now bowing and bending low.

What tale do the roaring ocean,
   And the night-wind, bleak and **wild,**
As they beat at the crazy casement,
   Tell to that little child?

And why do the roaring ocean,
   And the night-wind, wild and bleak,
As they beat at the heart of the **mother,**
   Drive the color from her cheek?

SIR HUMPHREY GILBERT.

SOUTHWARD with fleet of ice
   Sailed the corsair Death ;
Wild and fast blew the blast,
   And the east-wind was his breath.

His lordly ships of ice
    Glisten in the sun;
On each side, like pennons wide,
    Flashing crystal streamlets run.

His sails of white sea-mist
    Dripped with silver rain;
But where he passed there were cast
    Leaden shadows o'er the main.

Eastward from Campobello
    Sir Humphrey Gilbert sailed;
Three days or more seaward he bore,
    Then, alas! the land-wind failed.

Alas! the land-wind failed,
    And ice-cold grew the night;
And nevermore, on sea or shore,
    Should Sir Humphrey see the light.

He sat upon the deck,
    The Book was in his hand;
" Do not fear!   Heaven is as near,"
    He said, " by water as by land!"

In the first watch of the night,
    Without a signal's sound,
Out of the sea, mysteriously,
    The fleet of Death rose all around.

The moon and the evening star
   Were hanging in the shrouds;
Every mast as it passed,
   Seemed to rake the passing clouds.

They grappled with their prize,
   At midnight black and cold!
As of a rock was the shock;
   Heavily the ground-swell rolled.

Southward through day and dark,
   They drift in close embrace,
With mist and rain, to the Spanish main;
   Yet there seems no change of place.

Southward, forever southward,
   They drift through dark and day;
And like a dream, in the Gulf-stream
   Sinking, vanish all away.

———

THE LIGHTHOUSE.

THE rocky ledge runs far into the sea,
   And on its outer point, some miles away,
The Lighthouse lifts its massive masonry,
   A pillar of fire by night, of cloud by day.

Even at this distance I can see the tides,
  Upheaving, break unheard along its base,
A speechless wrath, that rises and subsides
  In the white lip and tremor of the face.

And as the evening darkens, lo! how bright,
  Through the deep purple of the twilight air,
Beams forth the sudden radiance of its light
  With strange, unearthly splendor in its glare!

Not one alone; from each projecting cape
  And perilous reef along the ocean's verge,
Starts into life a dim, gigantic shape,
  Holding its lantern o'er the restless surge.

Like the great giant Christopher it stands
  Upon the brink of the tempestuous wave,
Wading far out among the rocks and sands,
  The night o'ertaken mariner to save.

And the great ships sail outward and return,
  Bending and bowing o'er the billowy swells,
And ever joyful, as they see it burn,
  They wave their silent welcomes and farewells.

They come forth from the darkness, and their
    sails
  Gleam for a moment only in the blaze,
And eager faces, as the light unveils,
  Gaze at the tower, and vanish while **they gaze.**

The mariner remembers when a child,
　On his first voyage, he saw it fade and sink,
And when, returning from adventures wild,
　He saw it rise again o'er ocean's brink.

Steadfast, serene, immovable, the same
　Year after year, through all the silent night
Burns on forevermore that quenchless flame,
　Shines on that inextinguishable light!

It sees the ocean to its bosom clasp
　The rocks and sea-sand with the kiss of peace;
It sees the wild winds lift it in their grasp,
　And hold it up, and shake it like a fleece.

The startled waves leap over it; the storm
　Smites it with all the scourges of the rain,
And steadily against its solid form
　Press the great shoulders of the hurricane.

The sea-bird wheeling round it, with the din
　Of wings and winds and solitary cries,
Blinded and maddened by the light within,
　Dashes himself against the glare, and dies.

A new Prometheus, chained upon the rock,
　Still grasping in his hand the fire of Jove,
It does not hear the cry, nor heed the shock,
　But hails the mariner with words of love.

"**Sail** on !" it says, "sail on, ye stately ships Ꞌ
   And with your floating bridge the ocean **span** ꞉
Be mine to guard this light from all eclipse,
   Be yours to bring man nearer unto **man** !"

THE FIRE OF DRIFT-WOOD.

DEVEREUX FARM, NEAR MARBLEHEAD.

WE sat within the farm-house old,
   Whose windows, looking o'er the bay,
Gave to the sea-breeze, damp and cold,
   An easy entrance, night and day.

Not far away we saw the port,
   The strange, old-fashioned, silent town,
The lighthouse, the dismantled fort,
   The wooden houses, quaint and brown.

We sat and talked until the night,
   Descending, filled the little room ;
Our faces faded from the sight,
   Our voices only broke the gloom.

We spake of many a vanished scene,
   Of what we once had thought and **said,**
Of what had been, and might have been,
   And who was changed, and who was **dead** ꞉

And all that fills the hearts of friends,
  When first they feel, with secret pain,
Their lives thenceforth have separate ends,
  And never can be one again;

The first slight swerving of the heart,
  That words are powerless to express,
And leave it still unsaid in part,
  Or say it in too great excess.

The very tones in which we spake
  Had something strange, I could but mark;
The leaves of memory seemed to make
  A mournful rustling in the dark.

Oft died the words upon our lips,
  As suddenly, from out the fire
Built of the wreck of stranded ships,
  The flames would leap and then expire,

And, as their splendor flashed and failed,
  We thought of wrecks upon the main,
Of ships dismasted, that were hailed
  And sent no answer back again.

The windows, rattling in their frames,
  The ocean, roaring up the beach,
The gusty blast, the bickering flames,
  All mingled vaguely in our speech;

Until they made themselves a part
  Of fancies floating through the brain,
The long-lost ventures of the heart,
  That send no answers back again.

O flames that glowed! O hearts that yearned!
  They were indeed too much akin,
The drift-wood fire without that burned,
  The thoughts that burned and glowed within.

BY THE FIRESIDE.

BY THE FIRESIDE.

RESIGNATION.

THERE is no flock, however watched and tended,
   But one dead lamb is there!
There is no fireside, howsoe'er defended,
   But has one vacant chair!

The air is full of farewells to the dying,
   And mournings for the dead;
The heart of Rachel, for her children crying,
   Will not be comforted!

Let us be patient!   These severe afflictions
   Not from the ground arise,
But oftentimes celestial benedictions
   Assume this dark disguise.

We see but dimly through the mists and vapors;
   Amid these earthly damps,
What seem to us but sad, funereal tapers
   May be heaven's distant lamps.

There is no Death!   What seems so is transition;
   This life of mortal breath

331

Is but a suburb of the life elysian,
    Whose portal we call Death.

She is not dead, — the child of our affection, —
    But gone unto that school
Where she no longer needs our poor protection,
    And Christ himself doth rule.

In that great cloister's stillness and seclusion,
    By guardian angels led,
Safe from temptation, safe from sin's pollution,
    She lives, whom we call dead.

Day after day we think what she is doing
    In those bright realms of air;
Year after year, her tender steps pursuing,
    Behold her grown more fair.

Thus do we walk with her, and keep unbroken
    The bond which nature gives,
Thinking that our remembrance, though un-
    spoken,
    May reach her where she lives.

Not as a child shall we again behold her;
    For when with raptures wild
In our embraces we again enfold her,
    She will not be a child;

But a fair maiden, in her Father's mansion,
    Clothed with celestial grace;

"Stretches the desert with its shifting sand,
Its unimpeded sky."

And beautiful with all the soul's expansion
   Shall we behold her face.

And though at times impetuous with emotion
   And anguish long suppressed,
The swelling heart heaves moaning like the ocean,
   That cannot be at rest, —

We will be patient, and assuage the feeling
   We may not wholly stay;
By silence sanctifying, not concealing,
   The grief that must have way.

THE BUILDERS.

   ALL are architects of Fate,
      Working in these walls of Time;
   Some with massive deeds and great,
      Some with ornaments of rhyme.

   Nothing useless is, or low;
      Each thing in its place is best;
   And what seems but idle show
      Strengthens and supports the rest.

   For the structure that we raise,
      Time is with materials filled;
   Our to-days and yesterdays
      Are the blocks with which we build.

Truly shape and fashion these;
  Leave no yawning gaps between;
Think not, because no man sees,
  Such things will remain unseen.

In the elder days of Art,
  Builders wrought with greatest care
Each minute and unseen part;
  For the Gods see everywhere.

Let us do our work as well,
  Both the unseen and the seen;
Make the house, where Gods may dwell,
  Beautiful, entire, and clean.

Else our lives are incomplete,
  Standing in these walls of Time,
Broken stairways, where the feet
  Stumble as they seek to climb.

Build to-day, then, strong and sure,
  With a firm and ample base;
And ascending and secure
  Shall to-morrow find its place.

Thus alone can we attain
  To those turrets, where the eye
Sees the world as one vast plain,
  And one boundless reach of sky.

SAND OF THE DESERT IN AN HOUR-GLASS.

A HANDFUL of red sand, from the hot clime
    Of Arab deserts brought,
Within this glass becomes the spy of Time,
    The minister of Thought.

How many weary centuries has it been
    About those deserts blown!
How many strange vicissitudes has seen,
    How many histories known!

Perhaps the camels of the Ishmaelite
    Trampled and passed it o'er,
When into Egypt from the patriarch's sight
    His favorite son they bore.

Perhaps the feet of Moses, burnt and bare,
    Crushed it beneath their tread;
Or Pharaoh's flashing wheels into the air
    Scattered it as they sped;

Or Mary, with the Christ of Nazareth
    Held close in her caress,
Whose pilgrimage of hope and love and faith
    Illumed the wilderness;

Or anchorites beneath Engaddi's palms
    Pacing the Dead Sea beach,

And singing slow their old Armenian psalms
    In half-articulate speech;

Or caravans, that from Bassora's gate
    With westward steps depart;
Or Mecca's pilgrims, confident of Fate,
    And resolute in heart!

These have passed over it, or may have passed!
    Now in this crystal tower
Imprisoned by some curious hand at last,
    It counts the passing hour.

And as I gaze, these narrow walls expand;
    Before my dreamy eye
Stretches the desert with its shifting sand,
    Its unimpeded sky.

And borne aloft by the sustaining blast,
    This little golden thread
Dilates into a column high and vast,
    A form of fear and dread.

And onward, and across the setting sun,
    Across the boundless plain,
The column and its broader shadow run,
    Till thought pursues in vain.

The vision vanishes! These walls again
    Shut out the lurid sun,
Shut out the hot, immeasurable plain;
    The half-hour's sand is run!

" This is the cry
  Of souls, that high
  On toiling, beating pinions fly,
Seeking a warmer clime."

BIRDS OF PASSAGE.

BLACK shadows fall
From the lindens tall,
That lift aloft their massive wall
 Against the southern sky;

And from the realms
Of the shadowy elms
A tide-like darkness overwhelms
 The fields that round us lie.

But the night is fair,
And everywhere
A warm, soft vapor fills the air,
 And distant sounds seem near;

And above, in the light
Of the star-lit night,
Swift birds of passage wing their flight
 Through the dewy atmosphere.

I hear the beat
Of their pinions fleet,
As from the land of snow and sleet
 They seek a southern lea.

I hear the cry
Of their voices high
Falling dreamily through the sky,
 But their forms I cannot see.

337

O, say not so!
Those sounds that flow
In murmurs of delight and **woe**
   Come not from wings of birds.

They are the throngs
Of the poet's songs,
Murmurs of pleasures, and pains, **and wrongs,**
   The sound of wingèd words.

This is the cry
Of souls, that high
On toiling, beating pinions, fly,
   Seeking a warmer clime.

From their distant flight
Through realms of light
It falls into our world of night,
   With the murmuring sound of **rhyme.**

———

THE OPEN WINDOW.

The old house by the lindens
   Stood silent in the shade,
And on the gravelled pathway
   The light and shadow played.

I saw the nursery windows
   Wide open to the air;

338

But the faces of the children,
　　They were no longer there.

The large Newfoundland house-dog
　　Was standing by the door;
He looked for his little playmates,
　　Who would return no more.

They walked not under the lindens,
　　They played not in the hall;
But shadow, and silence, and sadness
　　Were hanging over all.

The birds sang in the branches,
　　With sweet, familiar tone;
But the voices of the children
　　Will be heard in dreams alone!

And the boy that walked beside me,
　　He could not understand
Why closer in mine, ah! closer,
　　I pressed his warm, soft hand!

————

KING WITLAF'S DRINKING-HORN.

WITLAF, a king of the Saxons,
　　Ere yet his last he breathed,
To the merry monks of Croyland
　　His drinking-horn bequeathed,—

That, whenever they sat at their revels,
  And drank from the golden bowl,
They might remember the donor,
  And breathe a prayer for his soul.

So sat they once at Christmas,
  And bade the goblet pass;
In their beards the red wine glistened
  Like dew-drops in the grass.

They drank to the soul of Witlaf,
  They drank to Christ the Lord,
And to each of the Twelve Apostles,
  Who had preached his holy word.

They drank to the Saints and Martyrs
  Of the dismal days of yore,
And as soon as the horn was empty
  They remembered one Saint more.

And the reader droned from the pulpit,
  Like the murmur of many bees,
The legend of good Saint Guthlac
  And Saint Basil's homilies;

Till the great bells of the convent,
  From their prison in the tower,
Guthlac and Bartholomæus,
  Proclaimed the midnight hour.

And the Yule-log cracked in the chimney,
  And the Abbot bowed his head,
And the flamelets flapped and flickered,
  But the Abbot was stark and dead.

Yet still in his pallid fingers
  He clutched the golden bowl,
In which, like a pearl dissolving,
  Had sunk and dissolved his soul.

But not for this their revels
  The jovial monks forbore,
For they cried, "Fill high the goblet!
  We must drink to one Saint more!"

GASPAR BECERRA.

By his evening fire the artist
  Pondered o'er his secret shame;
Baffled, weary, and disheartened,
  Still he mused, and dreamed of fame.

'Twas an image of the Virgin
  That had tasked his utmost skill;
But, alas! his fair ideal
  Vanished and escaped him still.

341

From a distant Eastern island
   Had the precious wood been brought;
Day and night the anxious master
   At his toil untiring wrought;

Till, discouraged and desponding,
   Sat he now in shadows deep,
And the day's humiliation
   Found oblivion in sleep.

Then the voice cried, " Rise, O master!
   From the burning brand of oak
Shape the thought that stirs within thee!"
   And the startled artist woke. —

Woke, and from the smoking embers
   Seized and quenched the glowing wood;
And therefrom he carved an image,
   And he saw that it was good.

O thou sculptor, painter, poet!
   Take this lesson to thy heart:
That is best which lieth nearest;
   Shape from that thy work of art.

PEGASUS IN POUND.

ONCE into a quiet village,
    Without haste and without heed,
In the golden prime of morning,
    Strayed the poet's wingèd steed.

It was Autumn, and incessant
    Piped the quails from shocks and sheaves,
And, like living coals, the apples
    Burned among the withering leaves.

Loud the clamorous bell was ringing
    From its belfry gaunt and grim;
'Twas the daily call to labor,
    Not a triumph meant for him.

Not the less he saw the landscape,
    In its gleaming vapor veiled;
Not the less he breathed the odors
    That the dying leaves exhaled.

Thus, upon the village common,
    By the schoolboys he was found;
And the wise men, in their wisdom,
    Put him straightway into pound.

Then the sombre village crier,
    Ringing loud his brazen bell,
Wandered down the street proclaiming
    There was an estray to sell.

343

And the curious country people,
　　Rich and poor, and young and old,
Came in haste to see this wondrous
　　Wingèd steed, with mane of gold.

Thus the day passed, and the evening
　　Fell, with vapors cold and dim;
But it brought no food nor shelter,
　　Brought no straw nor stall, for him.

Patiently, and still expectant,
　　Looked he through the wooden bars,
Saw the moon rise o'er the landscape,
　　Saw the tranquil, patient stars;

Till at length the bell at midnight
　　Sounded from its dark abode,
And, from out a neighboring farm-yard,
　　Loud the cock Alectryon crowed.

Then, with nostrils wide distended,
　　Breaking from his iron chain,
And unfolding far his pinions,
　　To those stars he soared again.

On the morrow, when the village
　　Woke to all its toil and care,
Lo! the strange steed had departed,
　　And they knew not when nor where.

But they found, upon the greensward
   Where his struggling hoofs had trod,
Pure and bright, a fountain flowing
   From the hoof-marks in the sod.

From that hour, the fount unfailing
   Gladdens the whole region round,
Strengthening all who drink its waters,
   While it soothes them with its sound.

———

TEGNÉR'S DEATH.

I HEARD a voice, that cried,
" Balder the Beautiful
Is dead, is dead ! "
And through the misty air
Passed like the mournful cry
Of sunward sailing cranes.

I saw the pallid corpse
Of the dead sun
Borne through the Northern sky.
Blasts from Niffelheim
Lifted the sheeted mists
Around him as he passed.

And the voice forever cried,
" Balder the Beautiful
Is dead, is dead ! "
And died away
Through the dreary night,
In accents of despair.

Balder the Beautiful,
God of the summer sun,
Fairest of all the Gods !
Light from his forehead beamed,
Runes were upon his tongue,
As on the warrior's sword.

All things in earth and air
Bound were by magic spell
Never to do him harm ;
Even the plants and stones ;
All save the mistletoe,
The sacred mistletoe !

Hœder, the blind old God,
Whose feet are shod with silence,
Pierced through that gentle breast
With his sharp spear, by fraud
Made of the misletoe,
The accursed misletoe !

They laid him in his ship,
With horse and harness,
As on a funeral pyre.
Odin placed
A ring upon his finger,
And whispered in his ear.

They launched the burning **ship!**
It floated far away
Over the misty sea,
Till like the sun it seemed,
Sinking beneath the waves.
Balder returned no more!

So perish the old Gods!
But out of the sea of **Time**
Rises a new land of song,
Fairer than the old.
Over its meadows green
Walk the young bards and **sing.**

Build it again,
O ye bards,
Fairer than before!
Ye fathers of the new **race,**
Feed upon morning dew,
Sing the new Song of Love!

SONNET.

The law of force is dead!
The law of love prevails!
Thor, the thunderer,
Shall rule the earth no more.
No more, with threats,
Challenge the meek Christ.

Sing no more,
O ye bards of the North,
Of Vikings and of Jarls!
Of the days of Eld
Preserve the freedom only,
Not the deeds of blood!

SONNET.

ON MRS. KEMBLE'S READINGS FROM SHAKESPEARE.

O PRECIOUS evenings! all too swiftly sped!
    Leaving us heirs to amplest heritages
    Of all the best thoughts of the greatest sages,
    And giving tongues unto the silent dead!
How our hearts glowed and trembled as she read,
    Interpreting by tones the wondrous pages
    Of the great poet who foreruns the ages,
    Anticipating all that shall be said!
O happy Reader! having for thy text

348

The magic book, whose Sibylline leaves **have**
    caught
The rarest essence of all human thought !
O happy Poet ! by no critic vext !
    How must thy listening spirit now rejoice
    To be interpreted by such a voice !

———

THE SINGERS.

GOD sent his Singers upon earth
With songs of sadnesss and of mirth,
That they might touch the hearts of men,
And bring them back to heaven again.

The first, a youth, with soul of fire,
Held in his hand a golden lyre ;
Through groves he wandered, and by **streams,**
Playing the music of our dreams.

The second, with a bearded face,
Stood singing in the market-place,
And stirred with accents deep and loud
The hearts of all the listening crowd.

A gray old man, the third and last,
Sang in cathedrals dim and vast,
While the majestic organ rolled
Contrition from its mouths of gold.

And those who heard the Singers three
Disputed which the best might be;
For still their music seemed to start
Discordant echoes in each heart.

But the great Master said, "I see
No best in kind, but in degree;
I gave a various gift to each,
To charm, to strengthen, and to teach.

"These are the three great chords of might,
And he whose ear is tuned aright
Will hear no discord in the three,
But the most perfect harmony."

SUSPIRIA.

TAKE them, O Death! and bear away
   Whatever thou canst call thine own!
Thine image, stamped upon this clay,
   Doth give thee that, but that alone!

Take them, O Grave! and let them lie
   Folded upon thy narrow shelves,
As garments by the soul laid by,
   And precious only to ourselves!

Take them, O great Eternity!
    Our little life is but a gust
That bends the branches of thy tree,
    And trails its blossoms in the dust!

———

HYMN

FOR MY BROTHER'S ORDINATION.

CHRIST to the young man said : " Yet one thing
        more ;
    If thou wouldst perfect be,
Sell all thou hast and give it to the poor,
    And come and follow me ! "

Within this temple Christ again, unseen,
    Those sacred words hath said,
And his invisible hands to-day have been
    Laid on a young man's head.

And evermore beside him on his way
    The unseen Christ shall move,
That he may lean upon his arm and say,
    " Dost thou, dear Lord, approve ? "

Beside him at the marriage feast shall be,
    To make the scene more fair ;

351

Beside him in the dark Gethsemane
  Of pain and midnight prayer.

O holy trust!   O endless sense of rest!
  Like the beloved John
To lay his head upon the Saviour's breast,
  And thus to journey on!